PEOPLE & PLACES

Greece

Written by

Bridget and Neil Ardley

Consultant Dr. Kypros Tofallis

Illustrated by

Ann Savage

SILVER BURDETT PRESS
ENGLEWOOD CLIFFS, NEW JERSEY

WHERE IN THE WORLD?

Greece, which the Greek people call the Hellenic Republic, is about the same size as the state of Alabama and slightly larger than England. It is in southern Europe at the tip of the Balkan peninsula, jutting out into the Mediterranean Sea. To the north and east, Greece has borders with Albania, Yugoslavia, Bulgaria, and Turkey.

The coast of Greece has many inlets, and no part of the country is more than 85 miles from the sea. About four-fifths of Greece is covered by mountains. Islands make up about 20 percent of the area of the country and 169 of these have people living on them. Over 1,000 Greek islands are uninhabited.

The southern part of Greece has a Mediterranean climate, which means that the summer is usually hot and dry and the winter warm and wet. In the northern mountainous regions, however, it is often freezing cold in winter and snow may fall.

Most Greek people live on the mainland. About half of them live in the major cities, especially in the capital, Athens. Many are leaving the villages and islands to go to the cities to find work.

Greece is a member of the European Economic Community (EEC) and plays an important part in European affairs.

Proud *evzones*
These colorful soldiers called evzones guard the parliament of Greece and the president's palace in Athens. They also take part in ceremonies.

Symbols of Greece

The blue stripes on the Greek flag represent the sea and the sky, and the white stripes stand for the Greek struggle for independence. The white cross in the top left corner represents the Greek Orthodox Church.

The Parthenon stands on top of a high rock called the Acropolis in Athens, and is one of the best-known buildings in the world. It was built almost 2,500 years ago as a temple to the goddess Athena.

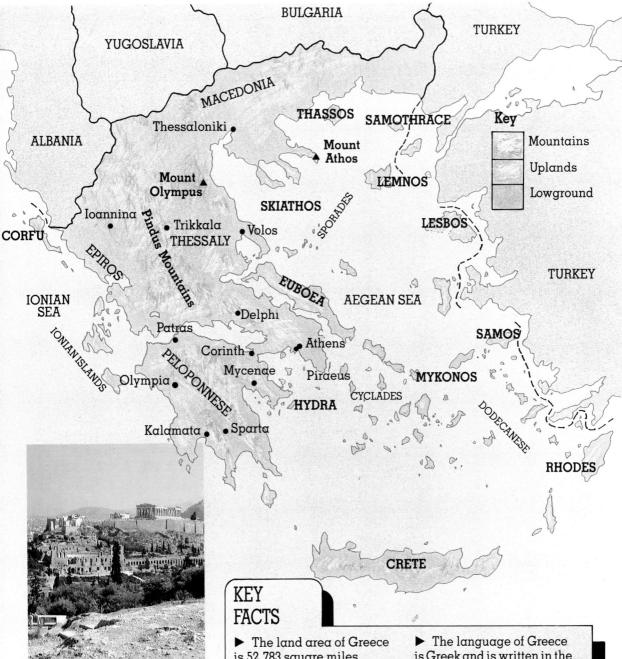

Key

	Mountains
	Uplands
	Lowground

BULGARIA

TURKEY

YUGOSLAVIA

MACEDONIA

ALBANIA

Thessaloniki

THASSOS

SAMOTHRACE

Mount Athos

LEMNOS

Mount Olympus

Ioannina

SKIATHOS

SPORADES

LESBOS

CORFU

Trikkala
THESSALY

Volos

EPIROS

Pindus Mountains

EUBOEA

AEGEAN SEA

TURKEY

IONIAN SEA

Delphi

Patras

SAMOS

Corinth

Athens

IONIAN ISLANDS

PELOPONNESE

Mycenae

Piraeus

MYKONOS

Olympia

HYDRA

CYCLADES

DODECANESE

Kalamata

Sparta

RHODES

CRETE

Athens

People began to live in the region of Athens nearly 5,000 years ago. It became the capital of an area called Attica over 2,500 years ago. It was made the capital of present-day Greece in 1834.

KEY FACTS

▶ The land area of Greece is 52,783 square miles.
▶ The population of Greece is over 9,964,000.
▶ Athens, the capital and largest city, has a population of over three million.
▶ Greece is divided into 52 regions called *nomoi*, for local government.

▶ The language of Greece is Greek and is written in the Greek alphabet. It has two forms: *katharevousa* and *dimotiki*.
▶ The main religion is the Greek Orthodox Church.
▶ The unit of currency is the *drachma*, which is divided into 100 *lepta*.

7

MOUNTAINS AND ISLANDS

Rugged mountains cover most of the mainland of Greece, and many of the islands are the tops of mountains that sank into the sea long ago. The Gulf of Corinth almost divides the mainland into two separate parts. Only a narrow neck of land links the southern part, the Peloponnese, to the rest of mainland Greece. The main range of mountains, the Pindus Mountains, runs through northern and central Greece, from Thessaly to Albania. Its highest peak rises to more than 8,054 feet. Among the mountains are some fertile valleys and plains, watered by rivers. However, many rivers dry up in summer because there is very little rain.

The parts of the Mediterranean Sea around mainland Greece are called the Ionian Sea to the west and the Aegean Sea to the east. No one knows for certain exactly how many islands there are in Greece, but there may be as many as 2,000. Some are green and fertile, but many are dry, rocky, and mountainous. Crete is the largest island, lying in the southern part of the Aegean Sea.

Greece suffers from severe earthquakes. The most recent struck the city of Kalamata, in the Peloponnese, in 1986, causing great damage. Shortly after World War 1 even more severe earthquakes leveled Cephalonia, in the Ionian islands, and Volos, on the east coast of Greece.

The Corinth Canal
The Corinth Canal crosses the neck of land joining the Peloponnese to the rest of mainland Greece. It was opened in 1893. Ships use the canal to get from Athens to the western Mediterranean without having to sail all the way around the Peloponnese.

A huge breadbasket
Thessaly is a region of east-central Greece. It consists of a large fertile plain surrounded by mountains. So much wheat is grown in this area that it is sometimes called the "breadbasket" of Greece.

Volcanic Santorini

The island of Santorini, also called Thira, is the remains of an enormous volcano that erupted in about 1645 BC. The island's high cliffs are the walls of this crater. Perched on top of these cliffs are white towns and villages. Santorini suffered a severe earthquake in 1956.

Home of the gods

Mount Olympus, in north Thessaly, is the highest mountain in Greece at 9,573 feet. In ancient times, it was believed to be the home of the gods. Snow lies on its summit for most of the year.

A LAND OF FLOWERS

I n spring and early summer, Greece blooms with hundreds of different wildflowers. Carpets of many colors cover even the driest hills and rocky mountains. Greece has a greater variety of wildflowers than any other country in Europe. Herbs such as thyme, sage, and oregano, which are used in cooking, spring up everywhere.

Many trees grow too, especially oleanders, with their pink and white blossoms. Cypresses, pines, junipers, and sweet chestnuts are also part of the landscape. Over the centuries, millions of olive trees have been planted in Greece. Figs, pomegranates, oranges, lemons, and vines are also common.

In some of the wilder areas of Greece, wild boar, wolves, lynx, wild goats, and bears remain, though in small numbers. Tortoises are often seen both on the mainland and the islands, and the hawksbill turtle lays its eggs on the island of Zakynthos. Lizards are active in summer, and the constant chirping of cicadas fills the air. Eagles and storks can be seen in the sky, and pelicans on the seashore.

Wildflowers
When the hot summer sun shines, the vegetation dries up. It flowers again the following spring.

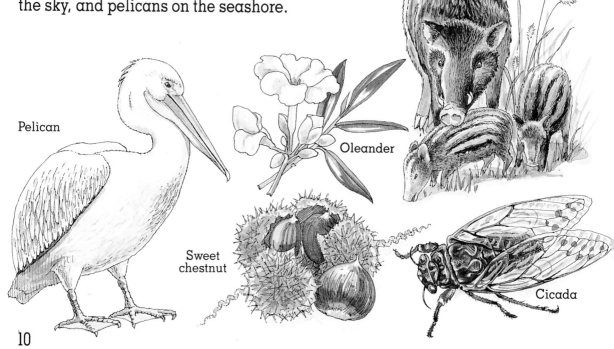

Wild boar

Pelican

Oleander

Sweet chestnut

Cicada

Temple of Olympian Zeus
This great temple in Athens was started in the 6th century BC, but was not completed until 700 years later by the Roman emperor Hadrian. It originally had 104 columns, but only 14 of them are standing today.

Mistra
Mistra, near Sparta, was an important Byzantine city. Today ruined houses, churches, monasteries, and palaces can be seen there. The churches have fine wall-paintings that reflect the great skill of the artists of the Byzantine period. Greek churches are still built in the Byzantine style.

UNDER TURKISH RULE

O nce the Turks had captured Constantinople in the 15th century, they swept across Greece. Only the Ionian Islands, which were ruled by Venice, escaped Turkish domination, and the Turks and Venetians warred for many years. The Turks treated the Greeks as second-class citizens, making each family give up a son to become a Turkish soldier. Many of the Turkish rulers were very cruel. However, the Greeks were allowed to follow their own religion.

During the 18th century, the Greeks began to look toward independence from their Turkish masters. They had a renewed interest and pride in their ancient past. In 1814 a group of Greek merchants in Russia organized a movement against the Turks. This movement led to the Greek Revolution of 1821.

In 1822 Greek independence was declared at Epidaurus. During the fighting that followed, many thousands were killed. In 1827 France, Great Britain, and Russia intervened and destroyed a combined Turkish and Egyptian fleet at the Battle of Navarino. The Turks left Greece in 1828 to fight the Russians. The Egyptians, who had been helping the Turks, left in 1829.

On September 14, 1829, by the Treaty of Adrianople, Greece became an independent nation.

The first president
Ioannis Capodistrias was born on Corfu in 1776. He went to Russia, where he became a foreign minister. In 1822 he returned to Greece to help in the fight for independence. In 1827 he was elected the first president of independent Greece.

"The Lion"
Albanian Ali Pasha was appointed by the Sultan of Turkey to rule Epiros, in the northwest of Greece. Known as the "Lion", he is remembered for his extreme cruelty. He rebelled against the Sultan in 1820 and was killed at Ioannina.

Siege at Missolonghi

The town of Missolonghi, to the west of Delphi, was besieged by the Turks and occupied from May 1825 to April 1826. The inhabitants tried to escape, but most were killed. Those remaining blew themselves up rather than be captured. The British poet Lord Byron died of a fever at Missolonghi while fighting for the Greeks.

Lord Byron

The Battle of Navarino

On October 20, 1827, a combined fleet of Russian, French, and British ships entered Navarino Bay in the Peloponnese. The Turkish-Egyptian fleet was destroyed in the battle.

17

THE KINGDOM OF GREECE

I n 1831 President Capodistrias was assassinated and civil war broke out. The European powers chose Prince Otto of Bavaria to be king of Greece in 1832. A revolt in 1843 forced Otto to set up a parliamentary government, but another rebellion removed him in 1862. A Danish prince became King George I of Greece in 1863. He reigned for 50 years.

Parts of Greece were still under Turkish rule. Various uprisings took place, especially in Crete, until the Balkan Wars of 1912-1913 won most of the disputed areas for Greece. In 1922 there was a further war with Turkey which left the border situation unresolved.

From 1914, there was much conflict inside Greece. Two kings were deposed and there was a republic (a form of government with a president rather than a king) from 1924 until 1935. In 1936 a dictatorship was established under General Ioannis Metaxas.

Greece held off an Italian invasion in 1940 at the start of World War II, but was invaded by Germany in 1941. When the Germans left in 1944, the communist resistance movement tried to take over. A civil war was fought from 1946 to 1949, between the communists and the royalists. With U.S. aid, the royalists won. In 1949 the monarchy was restored under King Paul. He was succeeded by his son Constantine in 1964. Constantine had a disagreement with his ministers, and in 1967 military leaders known as the Colonels took control.

KEY FACTS

▶ The new independent Greece in 1829 covered less than half the area of present-day Greece.
▶ Greece's desire to control all Greek territory under foreign rule was called the "Great Idea."
▶ Otto of Bavaria was only 17 years old when he was chosen to be king of Greece in 1832.
▶ The Ionian Islands were ruled by Venice and by France until 1815, when they became a British protectorate. In 1864 Great Britain handed them over to Greece.
▶ Between 1923 and 1930, more than a million Orthodox Greeks living in Turkey moved to Greece, while half a million Muslims living in Greece moved to Turkey.
▶ The last part of Greece to be returned from foreign rule was the Dodecanese Islands. Originally Greek, they were under Turkish rule until they were taken by Italy in 1912. Italy returned them to Greece in 1947.

Eleftherios Venizelos
The Cretan Venizelos became prime minister of Greece in 1910. He brought about many important changes. In 1914 he wanted Greece to join the Allies in World War 1 against Germany, but King Constantine I kept Greece neutral. After Constantine was deposed, Greece entered the war on the side of the Allies.

The Truman Doctrine

American president Harry S. Truman announced the Truman Doctrine in 1947. This meant that the United States would try to stop communist influence in Europe by supporting those who fought against it. As a result, the United States helped the Greek royalist forces against the communist-led rebels in 1949.

A heroic sacrifice

During the 19th century, there were uprisings against the Turks on Crete. In November 1866 a Turkish army tried to storm the monastery of Arkadi (the remains of which are shown here). Rather than allow it to be captured, the abbot ordered the monastery to be blown up. Everyone was killed, including 3,000 Turks. The heroic action is commemorated every year.

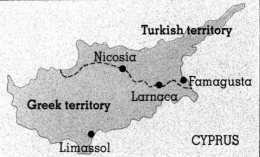

The Cyprus problem

During the 1950s, Greece and Turkey disagreed over the future of the island of Cyprus, which Great Britain had annexed when Turkey joined the First World War in 1914. After a period of severe tension, Cyprus became independent in 1960. In 1974 Turkey invaded northern Cyprus and occupied over a third of the island. A new state was declared in 1983, which only Turkey recognized. The United Nations continues to work toward a solution to this problem.

19

GREECE TODAY

During the period of military rule, the Colonels banned all political activity and allowed no opposition. Even the performance of ancient plays was banned. The king failed to overthrow the Colonels and was forced to leave the country. In 1973, Colonel George Papadopoulos declared Greece a republic with himself as president. Later, in 1973 Papadopoulos was overthrown and Lieutenant-General Phaidon Ghizikis became president.

In 1974 the failure to prevent the Turkish invasion of Cyprus caused the downfall of Greece's military government. Former prime minister Constantinos Karamanlis was recalled from exile to head a new civilian government, and military rule was ended. The Greek people voted against the return of the king and, in 1975, Greece became a republic. Karamanlis became president of Greece in 1980.

In 1981 Greece joined the European Economic Community. The elections of that year brought the socialist party PASOK to power and Andreas Papandreou became the first socialist prime minister. In 1986 the Greek constitution was altered, limiting the powers of the president.

Constantinos Karamanlis
Karamanlis has been prime minister of Greece four times. He left Greece in 1963, when he was accused of dishonesty in elections. The confusion that followed allowed the Colonels to take over. Karamanlis returned in triumph in 1974 to restore government by the people. He was president of Greece again from 1980 to 1985.

The Colonels seize power
On April 21, 1967, the Greek army took over the palace, all government offices and radio stations, and three officers took power. This group, called the *junta* or the Colonels, took away people's personal freedom, and controlled newspapers and the Church. Many people were arrested and thrown into prison. Everywhere, signs and slogans reminded people of the junta's power. This sign in Crete says "Long live the 21st of April."

King Constantine II

King Constantine remained head of state when the Colonels took over, but in name only. On December 13, 1967, he tried to overthrow the junta. He failed and had to flee to Italy with his family. In 1974 the Greek people voted against the return of the monarchy. Constantine has lived in exile ever since.

Political parties in Greece

Following the fall of the Colonels, various political parties began to emerge in Greece. The Panhellenic Socialist Movement (PASOK) was formed by Andreas Papandreou in 1974. The New Democracy party is a conservative group, and the Communist party of Greece is known as the KKE.

OLIVES AND GRAPES

Much of Greece is so dry and mountainous that not enough food can be grown to feed all the people. Only about a third of the land is suitable for growing crops. Half the remainder is used for grazing cattle, goats, and sheep. About a quarter of all working people work on the land.

Farmers grow cotton, tobacco, vegetables, and several kinds of fruit. Greece is a leading producer of lemons and of olives, which are turned into products such as olive oil. Grapes are used for making wine as well as for dried fruit like currants and raisins.

Greece imports much of its livestock, meat, and dairy products from abroad, but attempts are being made to improve home production. High-quality cattle and sheep from other countries are being used to breed better farm animals.

Rice is grown in some parts of Greece, even on types of soil that were once thought to be unfit for crops. A white cheese called *feta* is made from the milk of sheep and goats. Yogurt is another popular Greek dairy product.

Most Greek farms are small and the farmers use horses, mules, and donkeys, as well as tractors, to farm the land. There are about 200,000 donkeys and 90,000 mules in Greece.

A forest of lemons
The Lemonodasos — forest of lemon trees — is near Epidaurus, in the Peloponnese. Greece grows many lemons and other citrus fruits. In 1986 more than one million tons were produced.

Grazing in the mountains
In many of the wild mountainous areas, it is not possible to grow crops, so the villagers keep sheep and goats. Country people also raise bees for making honey. Greek honey is very popular because it is deliciously flavored by the many different flowers on which the bees feed.

Grape harvest
The whole family is harvesting the grapes on this farm in Crete. Many small farmers keep some of their grape crop to make their own wine. They sell the rest to a cooperative.

Olives everywhere
Olive trees are grown in all parts of Greece. The best olives are said to come from Kalamata, in the Peloponnese, and Amphissa, near Delphi. The olives may be stuffed with peppers or almonds and preserved in oil or brine. Greece makes excellent olive oil, which is exported to many other countries.

MINING AND MANUFACTURING

Greece has small amounts of minerals. A brown coal called lignite, used in power stations to produce electricity, is found there, but little ordinary coal. Bauxite, from which aluminum is made, is an important mineral found in Greece, as is chromite, from which chromium is made. Other minerals found there include iron pyrites, nickel, magnesite, barytes, and marble. There are small quantities of oil and natural gas.

Shipping is the major Greek industry, with tourism ranking the second most important. Manufacturing is increasing rapidly, but many goods have to be imported from abroad. Most factories are privately owned, and about three-fifths of all industry is in the area around Athens. Important Greek products include canned vegetables and fruit, textiles and clothing, chemicals, cement, glass, and porcelain.

Production of electricity has greatly increased in recent years. There are several hydroelectric plants in the Pindus Mountains. Now only about a quarter of villages do not have power, whereas before 1950 only about a quarter did have power. However, Greece needs more electricity to help increase its industry.

Polluted air

The large numbers of factories around Athens make the air very dirty. Fumes from motor vehicles add to this pollution, which is damaging to health as well as to the ancient buildings. The government is trying to clean up the factories and control the number of cars in the city.

Making cement

Cement-making is an important industry in Greece. Much of the cement is sold to other countries. It also is used to make concrete, of which most new houses and other buildings are constructed.

KEY FACTS

► In 1982 Greece produced nearly three million tons of bauxite.

► More than seven million tourists visit Greece each year.

► Piraeus, near Athens, is Greece's leading port.

► The country with which Greece does the most trading is West Germany.

► Greece buys about twice as many goods from other countries as she sells to them.

► Many Greeks living abroad send money home, which is a help to the Greek economy.

Marble

The Ancient Greeks used much marble in their buildings. Marble is still quarried in Greece today. The island of Paros was well known for its gleaming white marble, but this has all been used up. The main marble quarries are now at Penteli, just outside Athens.

A nation of sailors

Greece is almost surrounded by sea and has many islands, so the Greeks have always been seafarers. The Greek merchant fleet is the second largest in the world, after Japan. Greek ships sail the oceans of the world, working for Greece and for other countries.

VACATIONS IN THE SUN

Tourism earns a very large part of Greece's national income. It is the second largest industry after shipping.

When people first began to visit Greece, they mainly wanted to visit the ancient sites. Traveling to Greece was quite an adventure, as there were few hotels for visitors to stay in. However, since the 1950s, the tourist industry has grown rapidly. Many thousands of tourists visit the ancient ruins each year. Hotels have been built all over the country, even on the smallest islands. Beaches have been developed so that people can enjoy wind-surfing, sailing, and water-skiing, as well as swimming and sunbathing.

In the past, many Greeks had to go to other countries to find work, but now large numbers are employed in the tourist industry. They work in hotels and restaurants as well as in the thousands of craft and souvenir shops.

Tourist police
The tourist police force is responsible for looking after Greece's visitors. The officers are able to speak some foreign languages. They have to make sure that hotels and restaurants are clean and that they are charging correct prices. They also stop people from camping on beaches and in forests, where they might leave litter and start fires.

Historic Athens
Many people who visit Greece stay in Athens. One of the most popular sights is the Acropolis, where people see some of the finest Greek buildings. Parts of the buildings have been removed to museums to protect them from damage caused by pollution.

KEY FACTS

▶ In 1984 tourists spent more than $1.3 billion in Greece.

▶ 95 percent of all visitors to Greece go to Athens.

▶ Camping anywhere that is not a proper campsite is against the law in Greece.

▶ The National Tourist Organization of Greece (NTOG) provides help and information of all kinds to tourists.

▶ It is illegal to take anything, even a pebble, from an ancient site as a souvenir.

▶ In some places in Greece, old traditional houses have been restored by the NTOG and can be rented by tourists.

Mykonos

The island of Mykonos is one of Greece's most popular tourist resorts. Many of the Greeks who own hotels and restaurants there live in Athens in the winter. In spite of its popularity, the narrow streets of the enchanting town are still unspoiled.

Sun worshipers

Millions of visitors are attracted to Greece by the hot summer climate and the attractive beaches. The sea is often very clear, and snorkeling is popular. However, too many large hotels have spoiled several of the most beautiful beaches.

GETTING ABOUT IN GREECE

There are many cars in Greek cities. To lessen traffic jams and air pollution in Athens, cars can enter the city only on alternate days, depending on the numbers on their licence plates.

There are more than 22,000 miles of roads in Greece, and people use various means of travel, including cars, buses, trucks, and motorcycles. Railroads are much less important, and cover only about 1,550 miles.

People travel to and from the islands by means of ships and hydrofoils. The national airline, Olympic Airways, makes both national and international flights. Over eight and a half million people arrive at Athens airport each year. The hijacking of a TWA airliner from Athens in 1985 has led to greatly increased security at the airport.

In country areas, horses, and especially donkeys, are used for transportation. People ride donkeys because they are sure-footed and good at walking over rough, stony land. Donkeys may also carry large loads and can often be seen almost buried under piles of hay, grapes, or other crops.

Going by bus
Buses are one of the most popular means of transportation in Greece. Most towns and cities have more than one bus station, and you can go almost anywhere by bus. The buses, mostly run by a group called KTEL, are often decorated with lights, plastic flowers, icons, and pictures of the driver's family.

Donkey transportation
Farmers use sure-footed donkeys for transportation in the hilly, rocky countryside. On the island of Santorini, donkeys carry people up a flight of 600 steps from the harbor to the capital town, if they do not want to use the new cable railroad.

Kalavrita railroad

The railroad journey to Kalavrita, in the Peloponnese, is the most spectacular in Greece. It is a rack-and-pinion railroad. A large toothed wheel under the train fits into a toothed rail in the line, so that the train will not slip back on the steepest parts of the climb.

Hydrofoils

There is a hydrofoil service between Piraeus and some Greek islands. It is more expensive than traveling by ferry boat, but it is much faster and therefore more useful for business people.

29

LANGUAGE AND LEARNING

I t has been discovered that a written form of Greek was being used as long ago as 1400 BC. Most of the alphabets in Europe today are based on Greek letters. The word *alphabet* comes from the first two Greek letters, *alpha* and *beta*. Greek words are to be found in other languages. For example, English contains many Greek words, including *biology*, *architect*, and *music*.

Modern Greek looks very much like Ancient Greek when it is written, but it is put together and pronounced differently. There are two forms of the language. Until 1975, a written version called *katharevousa* was used for official purposes. *Demotiki*, the language that Greeks actually speak, has now become the official language, and this has been simplified.

Greeks enjoy reading newspapers. There are more than 30 daily papers in Athens alone and more than 100 elsewhere in the country.

All children in Greece must go to school between the ages of 6 and 15. Education is provided free at all stages by the government, but there are some private schools for which people must pay. Some rural areas are short of schools and teachers, but the number of people who cannot read and write has been reduced greatly in the past 30 years.

A	B	Γ	Δ	E	Z
α	β	γ	δ	ε	ζ
H	Θ	I	K	Λ	M
η	θ	ι	κ	λ	μ
N	Ξ	O	Π	P	Σ
ν	ξ	ο	π	ρ	σ
T	Y	Φ	X	Ψ	Ω
ι	υ	φ	χ	ψ	ω

The Greek alphabet
The Greek alphabet has 24 letters and many of the capital letters look different from the small (see chart above). In Greece many road signs are written in both the Greek alphabet and the Roman one — in which English is written. Greek letters are used as symbols in mathematics and science.

Ancient laws
This writing is carved on a building at Gortys, on the island of Crete, and is a list of ancient laws. It is written in a form of Greek called *boustrophedon*, which means "turning like oxen in ploughing." One line is written from left to right, the next goes from right to left, and so on.

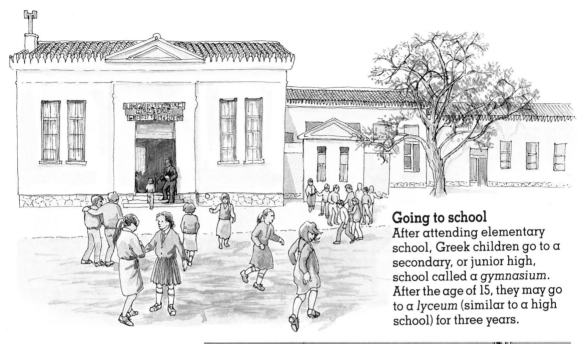

Going to school

After attending elementary school, Greek children go to a secondary, or junior high, school called a *gymnasium*. After the age of 15, they may go to a *lyceum* (similar to a high school) for three years.

University students

At one time, education at the secondary level was not advanced enough for people to get into a university easily. They had to go to special schools called *frondisteria* in order to prepare for the university. Now, however, school examinations help toward university entrance. Many students study medicine and law, but there is a need for more technical and scientific training. Shown here is Athens university.

31

MOTHER EARTH AND FATHER SKY

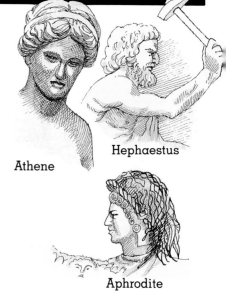

The Ancient Greeks believed that deities (gods and goddesses) watched over them and decided their fate. The goddess of Earth, Gaea or Ge, and Uranus, god of Heaven, were believed to be parents of giant Titans. One of the Titans was father of Zeus, chief of all the gods. There were a great many other deities related to one another, each responsible for a part of people's lives.

The Greeks also believed that the deities knew the future. The gods were believed to speak to priests and priestesses at special shrines called *oracles*. The most important oracle was at Delphi. Soldiers and even kings would alter their plans if the Delphic oracle warned of disaster.

Great temples were built where people worshiped the deities. People often had altars in their homes to honor gods and goddesses, offering them gifts of food and wine. They also held great festivals, which included games such as the Olympics.

In some ways, the gods were like ordinary people, showing anger, love, and jealousy. They were such an important part of everyday life that early Greek history sometimes seems to mix myths and legends of the gods and goddesses with real events.

Athene

Hephaestus

Aphrodite

Three Greek gods
Aphrodite was the goddess of love and beauty. Athene was goddess of wisdom and also of Athens. Stories say that she came out of Zeus' head after his skull was split by an ax. Hephaestus, god of fire, is supposed to have hit Zeus with the ax because he complained of a headache!

God of the sea
The temple of Poseidon, god of the sea, stands high on the cliffs at Cape Sounion, south of Athens on mainland Greece. Since ancient times, it has been a landmark for ships at sea.

Apart from the sea, Poseidon was also responsible for earthquakes, which he was believed to cause by shaking the earth with the forked trident that he always carried.

The center of the world

Ancient Greeks believed that Delphi was the center of the world. It was a shrine of the sun god Apollo and the most important oracle in Greece. People consulted the oracle about all kinds of things, such as whether to fight a battle or to build a city.

Brave heroes

Not all the people in Greek legends were gods. Heracles (or Hercules) was the son of Zeus and a human woman. He carried out twelve difficult tasks called Labors. The adventures of Ulysses and Achilles, who took part in the Trojan War, are told in the *Odyssey* by the poet Homer.

Heracles

Achilles

Ulysses

33

MUSIC AND THE ARTS

Mikis Theodorakis
The composer Mikis Theodorakis was imprisoned from 1967 to 1970 for trying to overthrow the Colonels. His music is well known in many countries. The film score that he composed for *Zorba the Greek* helped to popularize Greek music.

The artists of Ancient Greece left fine work, which is enjoyed by people today. Most of the painting is on pottery and on the walls of buildings. Sculptors like Phidias and Praxiteles carved statues. During the Byzantine period, mosaics decorated the churches and many holy pictures were painted. In the late 16th and early 17th centuries, a Cretan-born painter named Domenicos Theotocopoulos became known as El Greco, "The Greek." His paintings are known throughout the world.

The Ancient Greeks developed many forms of literature, such as poetry, drama, and comedy. People still enjoy reading the works of Homer, Pindar, Aeschylus, and many others. Popular Greek writers today include Nikos Kazantzakis and Costas Taktsis. Two poets, George Seferis and Odysseus Elytis, have won the Nobel Prize for literature in recent years.

Music has always been important in Greece. The English word *music* comes from the Greek *mousike*. Western music is based on the scales used in Ancient Greece. Important composers in Greece today include Manos Hadzidakis and Mikis Theodorakis. Much popular music features the *bouzouki*, a Greek lute. *Rembetika*, a type of traditional singing, has regained popularity.

Constantine Cavafy
Cavafy was the pen-name of Constantine Petrou (1862-1933). He is regarded as one of the great poets of the 20th century.

Homemade music

This man on the island of Paros is playing bagpipes that he has made himself from the skin of a goat. The boy's drum is also homemade. In the various parts of Greece, different kinds of instruments are used to play folk music, which often has an Eastern sound. An unusual three-string fiddle can be heard in Crete, for example.

The glory of Byzantium

The monastery at Daphni, near Athens, dates from the 11th century. It contains mosaics that are masterpieces of Byzantine art. A huge picture of Christ often appears inside the domes of Greek churches.

ARCHITECTURE AND BUILDINGS

The Ancient Greeks had skills and styles of building that influenced architecture in Europe and other parts of the world.

Cities had an *agora*, which was the shopping and business center. There were walled inner cities where great temples with tall columns stood. Open-air theaters were cleverly designed so that huge audiences could easily see and hear the action. Stadiums and racecourses were built.

The styles of architecture changed through different periods of history. The earliest examples can be seen at Knossos, on the island of Crete, and in Mycenae, in the Peloponnese. The ancient builders had some surprising skills. On the island of Samos, a water tunnel more than half a mile long was dug through solid rock in 524 BC.

The architecture of modern Greece mostly consists of buildings made of steel-reinforced concrete, rather than brick or wood, since many parts of the country and many islands suffer from earth tremors. However, traditional building styles can be seen, especially in the islands, and the people are very proud of their beautiful villages.

Beehive tombs
The tombs at Mycenae, near Athens, are amazing examples of the skill of ancient builders. They were built inside a hill, and have domed ceilings shaped like old-fashioned beehives. This is the high entrance to a beehive tomb.

Whitewashed buildings
The island of Mykonos has good examples of the style of architecture of the Cyclades Islands. Among the white cube-shaped houses is this typical church.

Doric (800-500 BC)　　　　　Ionic (500-338 BC)　　　　　Corinthian (338-146 BC)

Styles of architecture

The Ancient Greeks became very skilled at designing the columns that support their buildings. There were three basic styles that can be identified by the design at the top of the column. The Doric style was used from 800 to 500 BC; the Ionic until 338 BC; and the Corinthian lasted until the Romans arrived in 146 BC.

Stoa of Attalus

The excavation of the agora, the central marketplace of ancient Athens, was carried out by the American School of Classical Studies. The Stoa of Attalus, a covered walkway around the agora, cost $1,500,000 to reconstruct and is a fine example of how the city must have looked. The Stoa was lined with expensive shops. Fashionable Athenians must have enjoyed strolling among the elegant columns.

SAINTS AND HOLY PICTURES

Most Greeks belong to the Greek Orthodox Church. It is a Christian church headed by the archbishop of Athens. Orthodox churches are often very beautiful, and contain holy pictures called *icons*. When people pray to a particular saint for something, they often fix a small picture, representing their need, to the icon of the saint. Icons painted on the walls of old churches were put there to explain religious stories to people who could not read.

Christenings and weddings are carried out by priests, although since 1981 it has been possible to marry at a civil ceremony. An orthodox wedding is a very happy and informal celebration.

The most important religious festival is Easter, when open-air midnight services are held to mark the Resurrection of Christ. Every year, on August 15, at the Feast of the Assumption of the Virgin Mary, people flock to the island of Tinos. There a special icon of the Virgin is said to have been painted by St. Luke.

Orthodox priests
Unlike some Christian churches, the Greek Orthodox Church allows married men to become priests. Among religious communities in Greece, there is a very important one at Mount Athos in the northeast. The Holy Community consists of a group of 20 ancient monasteries. It has very strict rules, and women are forbidden to visit it.

The Church in Greece
The Orthodox Church owns much land in Greece, but the government has recently forced it to hand over unused agricultural land. The Church was very powerful at one time, but it no longer plays such an important part in people's lives. This tiny church in Athens is dwarfed by the office building that has been built over it.

Rice for good luck

At this wedding in a village near Delphi, the guests are throwing rice at the bride and groom to bring them luck, as the priest watches. After the wedding, the guests will be given gifts of sugared almonds and the bride and groom will lead dancing in the village square.

Monastery at Meteora

Monasteries and convents are often in remote places. At the Meteora, a group of giant rock pillars in central Greece, monks built their monasteries on the pinnacles of rock so that they could be alone and safe from their enemies. They used to climb up ladders or be pulled up in nets, but there are now stairs. The Varlaam monastery at the Meteora, shown here, was founded in 1517.

St. Spyridon

St. Spyridon is the patron saint of the island of Corfu. His mummified remains are carried around at festivals four times a year.

LIFE IN TOWN AND COUNTRY

Greek people start work very early in the day, while it is still cool. In the afternoon, when it is very hot, many people sleep and return to work later in the day. Both towns and villages often have a central square where people meet in the evenings. The men often carry small strings of beads called *komboloia*, which they click through their fingers as they say their prayers, or simply to pass the time.

Until fairly recently, Greek parents made all important decisions for their children, even when they were grown up. They would choose marriage partners, and a girl's family was expected to provide money or property, called a dowry, when she married. In the towns and cities, these customs have all but disappeared. Even in villages, family ties are far less strong than they used to be.

Greek people often eat out at restaurants. The food might include *moussaka*, made with aubergine and minced meat, and *souvlakia*, which is lamb grilled over charcoal. Sweet cakes made with honey and nuts are also popular.

The smallest shops
The kiosk, or *periptera*, is a familiar sight on the streets of Athens and other Greek cities. Kiosks sell almost everything you can think of, and often have public telephones as well. The kiosks were originally gifts from the state to wounded ex-soldiers so that they could earn a living. Now they are mostly owned by families.

A shepherd in Crete
In some rural areas, and on the islands, people still wear local costumes. This shepherd at Sfakia, on the island of Crete, is wearing a black scarf knotted around his head. Many people in this area say they wear black because they are in mourning for those who lost their lives fighting invaders in the past.

City life

While some people are hurrying about their business, others are sitting in the cafe enjoying each others' company. Some discuss politics, a favorite subject; others like to play backgammon.

Drying the octopus

These octopuses are hanging out to dry in the sun. Later they may be stewed, perhaps with wine and herbs, and eaten. Sometimes octopus is grilled over charcoal and served as part of *mezedes*, snacks that Greeks enjoy before their meals or with an aniseed-flavored drink called *ouzo*.

SPORTS AND LEISURE

Greece has a tradition of sports and games going back to ancient times. The most popular sport today is football. Basketball, volleyball, tennis, swimming, and skiing are also enjoyed, and on the island of Corfu, cricket is popular. A new Olympic stadium was completed in Athens in 1982.

Many people enjoy the theater, cinema, and concerts (see page 34). The annual Athens festival is staged at the Roman theater of Herod Atticus on the Acropolis. A modern open-air theater near the top of Mount Lycabettus in Athens often has concerts of Greek music. During festivals at Epidaurus and other ancient sites, Greek dramas are performed in the ancient theaters.

Traditional entertainment includes *karagiozi*, a shadow puppet theater which is also shown on television every week, and folk-dancing by troupes in colorful costumes.

Saints' days are often celebrated with a *panayiri*, when everyone gathers together for feasting and dancing. Greeks do not celebrate birthdays, but rather name days. These mark different saints' days. So, for example, if your name is Maria or John, you celebrate on those saints' days.

Cunning Karagiozis
The shadow puppet theater tells stories of Karagiozis, a poor but clever little man with an enormous arm that he uses to hit people on the head. The flat puppets are worked with rods behind a white screen.

A popular sport
Basketball is becoming more and more popular in Greece today.

Folk dancers

These dancers have been appearing at a festival on the island of Corfu. The dancers of Dora Stratou perform folk dances from all parts of Greece, wearing the costumes of each region. Many Greek people like to dance, and it is not unusual to see men dancing the *syrtaki* in cafes called *tavernas*.

The first marathon

The Greeks fought a battle against the Persians at Marathon in 490 BC. News of the Greek victory was taken to Athens by a runner. Today's marathon races commemorate that run.

TOMORROW'S GREECE

Greece is changing as the end of the 20th century approaches. Movement of people from the country may stop as new policies of the European Economic Community make country areas more prosperous.

Membership in the EEC means that Greece is trying to grow more crops to sell to other countries, so the old-style small farms may be replaced by larger ones. The Single European Market, which is to start in 1992, should benefit Greece. However, as factories start to use new machinery, the traditional craft industries are likely to disappear.

The tourist industry will continue to attract tourists. "Time-sharing," where visitors become part-owners of property, was made legal in Greece in 1986. Improvements in transportation will benefit the Greek people as well as the tourist industry.

In foreign affairs, Greece is trying to solve its disagreements with Turkey — for example, over drilling for oil in the Aegean Sea. The Cyprus situation remains tense as United Nations forces patrol the boundary between Greek and Turkish areas. At home, the Socialist government of Andreas Papandreou is threatened by scandals which may cause it to fall.

Modern city life
This is Omonia Square (right), near the center of Athens. It is one of the main squares in the city, with beautiful fountains, and is surrounded by shops and hotels. New buildings are going up everywhere in Greece — homes and factories as well as hotels for tourists.

Changing with the times
Greece's membership in the EEC has brought about changes in methods of production. This is because Greece is now able to sell more products to other countries.

Telecommunications
These satellite dishes on a
rocky hilltop in Crete are part
of Greece's modern
telecommunications network.
This network keeps the country
in touch with the rest of the
world.

Index

Acknowledgments

All illustrations by Ann Savage.
Photographic credits (a = above, b = below, m = middle, l = left, r = right):
All photographs by Neil Ardley, except page 19 b and 21 Popperfoto; page 25 R. Nicholas/Zefa; page 31 Robert Harding Picture Library; page 35 b Helbig/Zefa; page 45 a G. Ricatto/Zefa, b Robert Harding Picture Library.

HANDY HEALTH GUIDE TO COLDS AND FLU

Alvin and Virginia Silverstein
and Laura Silverstein Nunn

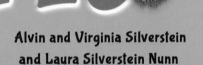

Enslow Publishers, Inc.
40 Industrial Road
Box 398
Berkeley Heights, NJ 07922
USA

http://www.enslow.com

Original edition published as *Common Colds* in 2001.

Library of Congress Cataloging-in-Publication Data
Silverstein, Alvin.
Handy health guide to colds and flu / by Alvin Silverstein, Virginia Silverstein, and Laura Silverstein Nunn.
pages cm. — (Handy health guides)
Includes bibliographical references and index.
  Summary: "An overview about colds and the flu--how germs are spread, how to treat these diseases, and how to avoid becoming sick"—Provided by publisher.
  ISBN 978-0-7660-4274-2
  1. Cold (Disease)—Juvenile literature. 2. Influenza—Juvenile literature. I. Silverstein, Virginia B. II. Nunn, Laura Silverstein. III. Title.
  RF361.S556 2014
  616.2'05—dc23
                                2012041450
Future editions:
Paperback ISBN: 978-1-4644-0491-7
EPUB ISBN: 978-1-4645-1254-4
Single-User PDF ISBN: 978-1-4646-1254-1
Multi-User PDF ISBN: 978-0-7660-5886-6

Printed in the United States of America

052013 Lake Book Manufacturing, Inc., Melrose Park, IL

10 9 8 7 6 5 4 3 2 1

To Our Readers: We have done our best to make sure all Internet Addresses in this book were active and appropriate when we went to press. However, the author and the publisher have no control over and assume no liability for the material available on those Internet sites or on other Web sites they may link to. Any comments or suggestions can be sent by e-mail to comments@enslow.com or to the address on the back cover.

♻ Enslow Publishers, Inc., is committed to printing our books on recycled paper. The paper in every book contains 10% to 30% post-consumer waste (PCW). The cover board on the outside of each book contains 100% PCW. Our goal is to do our part to help young people and the environment too!

Illustration Credits: 3D4Medical/Photo Researchers, Inc., p. 9; Aaron Haupt/Photo Researchers, Inc., p. 7; AP Images/NatiHarnik, p. 34; AP Images/Ross D. Franklin, p. 13; CDC, p. 19; dedMazay/Photos.com, p. 21; Douglas Jordan, M.A./CDC, p. 40; HiBlack/Photos.com, p. 24–25; @ iStockphoto.com/Sean Locke, p. 37; James Cavallini/Photo Researchers, Inc., p. 20; James Gathany/CDC, p. 39; Larisa Lofitskaya/Photos.com, p. 36; Shutterstock.com, pp. 1, 3, 4, 6, 11, 16, 17, 22, 23, 27, 28, 30, 31, 33, 38, 41, 42; Stockbyte/Photos.com, p. 15.

Cover Photo: Shutterstock.com

CONTENTS

Nobody likes
having a cold.
It can make you
sneeze, cough, and
have a runny nose

1

EVERYBODY GETS SICK!

Ah-choo! You know that miserable feeling. In fact, you may be having it right now. Your nose is so stuffed up, you can't breathe. You're coughing. You feel hot and tired and just plain awful!

Sounds like you have a cold—or is it the flu? People sometimes confuse the common cold with the flu, but the two illnesses feel very different.

Doctors call colds "common colds" because they happen so often, and to so many people. In fact, chances are that you or someone you know has had a cold in the past two weeks.

Colds are not very dangerous. People usually get better in about a week, even if they don't take medicine. But colds can make you feel miserable. People miss more days of school and work because of colds than for all other diseases combined!

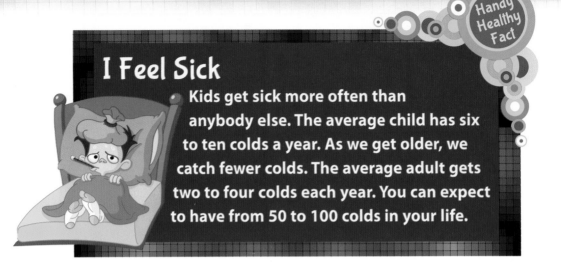

I Feel Sick

Kids get sick more often than anybody else. The average child has six to ten colds a year. As we get older, we catch fewer colds. The average adult gets two to four colds each year. You can expect to have from 50 to 100 colds in your life.

The flu is not as "common" as the common cold. Though millions of people come down with the flu each year, chances are you will get a lot more colds over your lifetime than you will get the flu.

When the flu hits you, though, its symptoms pack a powerful punch. They can make you feel so tired and achy you can't even get out of bed! Flu is also much more dangerous. It makes the body so weak that some people may wind up with another illness—and that may be life-threatening.

Why do we get sick more often when it is cold outside? In cold weather, people stay inside with the doors and windows closed and spend a lot of time with other people. This makes it easier for germs to move from one person to another. You can get a cold or the flu in the summer, too. And in tropical places, where it is hot all the time, people catch a lot of colds and flu. They get sick more often when it is rainy.

Can you tell the difference between a cold and the flu? What can you do to feel better when you get sick? Let's find out more about these illnesses.

Have you ever stayed home from school because you had a cold?

2

WHAT IS THE COMMON COLD?

The common cold is an illness that causes a stuffed-up, runny nose and a sore throat. It is caused by very tiny germs called viruses.

Viruses cannot live by themselves. They can live only inside a living animal or plant. The viruses that cause colds can live in the soft, wet lining inside a person's nose and throat. More than 200 different kinds of viruses can cause colds.

Viruses are much too small to see. In fact, you can't even see a virus with a magnifying glass or a typical microscope. Scientists need special electron microscopes to see a virus. Nobody even knew viruses existed until about a hundred years ago.

How small is a virus? Picture this: If a virus were as big as an ant, then you would be as big as the whole Earth!

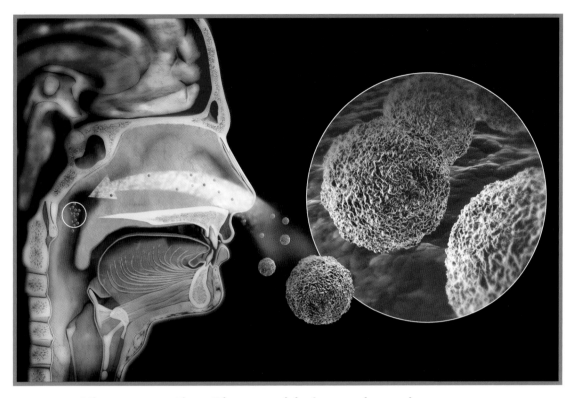

Viruses are tiny. These cold viruses have been magnified many times.

Viruses need to be inside people to make more viruses. They invade the cells in the lining of the nose and throat and turn the cells into virus-making factories. When a cell is full of viruses, it bursts open and the viruses spill out. The viruses are carried out of the body in the wet, slimy liquid that drips out. When you cough or sneeze, tiny droplets of liquid spray out and carry

Strange Ideas

Before people knew about viruses and other germs, they had some strange ideas about what caused illnesses. The ancient Greek doctor Hippocrates thought that colds were caused by waste matter in the brain. When the waste over-flowed, he said, it ran out the nose.

In the Middle Ages, people thought illnesses were caused by demons. They said that sneezing was very dangerous because a person's soul might be sneezed out, and a demon could sneak in and replace it. Saying "God bless you!" when people sneezed was a way to protect them from demons. Covering your nose and mouth when you sneezed could also protect you from demons.

viruses with them. When other people come into contact with these fluids, the viruses can invade their bodies, too. That's how viruses can spread from person to person.

By the time you feel a cold "coming on," you already have it. It can take up to two days after you are exposed to cold viruses for symptoms to develop. Colds often start off with a runny nose or a scratchy throat, then other symptoms may develop. You feel the worst after a few days and then you start feeling better until the symptoms are gone in a week or two. Bad colds are sometimes called "the flu," but the real flu is caused by a different group of viruses.

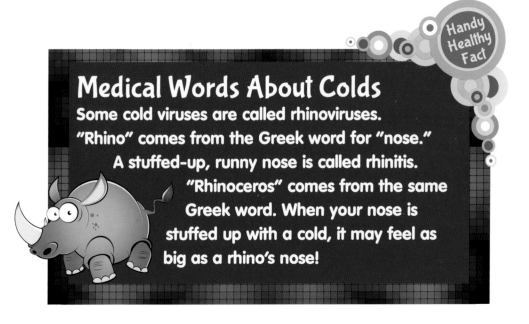

Handy Healthy Fact

Medical Words About Colds

Some cold viruses are called rhinoviruses. "Rhino" comes from the Greek word for "nose." A stuffed-up, runny nose is called rhinitis. "Rhinoceros" comes from the same Greek word. When your nose is stuffed up with a cold, it may feel as big as a rhino's nose!

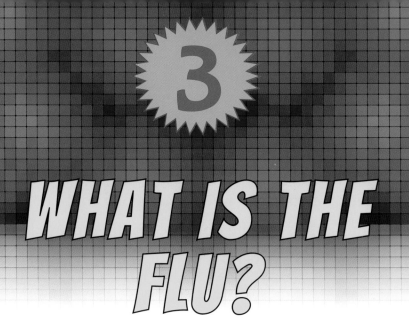

WHAT IS THE FLU?

Flu, short for influenza, is an illness that affects the respiratory system (the breathing passages and lungs). Its main symptoms are fever, chills, cough, extreme tiredness, muscle aches, and headaches. It is caused by viruses, but they are different from the ones that cause colds.

Only two main kinds of viruses can cause influenza: type A and type B. That's far fewer than the hundreds of cold viruses around. But the flu viruses are constantly changing. The flu that is "going around" one year is usually somewhat different from the ones that were around the year before.

In 2009, an unusual influenza virus—popularly called "swine flu"—was identified. This type A flu virus had commonly been seen in pigs but somehow spread to humans. A swine flu outbreak swept across the United States during the 2009–2010 flu season, affecting millions of people. Thousands of them had to be hospitalized, and some of them died from complications. The following year, the swine flu vaccine was combined with the regular flu vaccine for added protection.

Each year's flu vaccine is different. It contains the strain of flu that specialists believe will be the one that occurs most.

I've Got the Stomach Flu

When people are throwing up, they tend to say that they have the stomach flu. But this illness is not influenza. The two conditions are both caused by viruses, but not by the same kind. The influenza virus attacks the respiratory system. Stomach viruses attack the stomach and intestines. Their main symptoms are throwing up and diarrhea. Influenza rarely involves throwing up. Actually, the so-called "stomach flu" is most likely a form of food poisoning. People can get it by drinking or eating something that contains these viruses.

Medical experts do not like to use the term "stomach flu" because they believe it confuses people about what flu really is. The stomach virus is actually a milder illness, and its symptoms usually last for only twenty-four hours or so.

In the United States, flu season usually runs from October to May. Most cases seem to occur in late December and early March.

Flu can strike anyone at any age—from babies to the elderly. But schools are a great place for viruses to run wild, so usually families with school-age children are the first to be hit by the flu bug. Unlike colds, not everybody gets the flu every year. In fact many people go for years without catching it. Those who do get the flu rarely get it more than once in a year.

Kids in school can spread the flu easily. They may rub viruses from their noses and onto their hands, and then pass the virus to friends.

Is It a Cold or the Flu?

SYMPTOM	COLD	FLU
Fever	rare	high (102 F–104 F, lasts 3–4 days)
Headache	rare	usual
Aches/pains	slight	usual, often severe
Fatigue	mild	extreme, can last up to 2–3 weeks
Runny, stuffy nose	common	sometimes
Sneezing	common	sometimes
Sore throat	common	sometimes
Cough	mild to moderate	common, can become severe

When people are hit with the flu, they usually know it. Flu symptoms tend to come on suddenly, and can really wipe a person out in no time at all. Symptoms develop between one and four days after the person has been exposed to the flu virus. That means that people can spread the disease before they even know they have it.

For most people, the flu is not a dangerous illness. The symptoms can make you feel really bad—probably worse than any cold you've had. But eventually you will get better. For some people, though, the flu can become very serious, especially for babies, pregnant women, the elderly, and people with long-term health problems such as asthma, diabetes, or heart disease. People whose body defenses have been weakened by the flu may also develop other diseases, such as pneumonia.

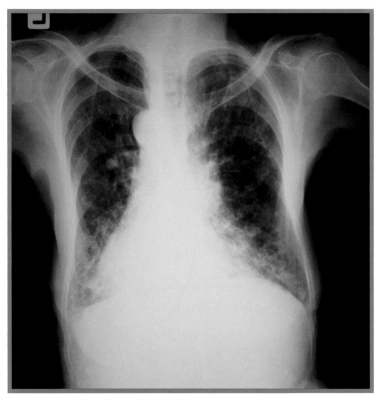

This X-ray shows shadowed areas in the lower area of this pneumonia patient's lungs.

17

The most serious complication of the flu is pneumonia, an infection of the lungs. Though some kinds of pneumonia are caused by viruses, the most dangerous cases of pneumonia are usually caused by bacteria. When these bacteria get past the body's defenses, they make their way into the lungs. There they can quickly multiply. Without immediate treatment, the infection can spread through the bloodstream and affect other parts of the body. So much damage may be done that the patient may die.

Every year, over 200,000 Americans wind up in the hospital from flu complications. And, each year, the flu is responsible for more than 30,000 deaths in the United States.

4

THE BODY DEFENDS ITSELF

The body has many defenses against germs. Cold or flu viruses that get into the mouth may be swept into the tonsils, where white blood cells are on patrol. Like good soldiers, the white cells surround germs and destroy them. Other viruses are swallowed. When they get down into the stomach, they are destroyed in a pool of acid.

The nose also has defenses against invading germs. Germs ride on dust particles and drops of liquid, which may be trapped by bristly hairs inside the nostrils. The germs that sneak

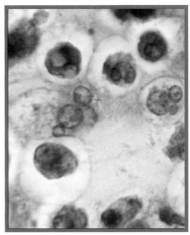

This is what your blood cells would look like if they were magnified more than 50,000 times.

past these hairs fall into the gooey fluid that covers the lining of the nose. This fluid is called mucus. The fluid flows along the lining, carrying the trapped germs toward the back of the throat. Then they may be swallowed. But the mucus does not move as fast when the air is cold and dry. Some viruses grab onto the outside of the cells and squirt some of their chemicals inside. These chemicals hold the instructions for making new cold viruses.

The cells that were invaded call for help. They use chemicals to call for the body's defenders. Some of the

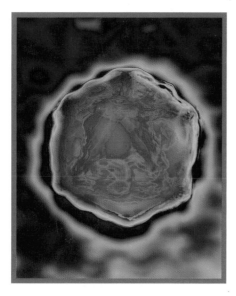

chemicals warn nearby cells about the viruses and help to protect them. Other chemicals call white blood cells. Still others make the lining leaky, so that the defending white cells can move more easily.

Viruses use the materials inside living cells to make more viruses. This rhinovirus is magnified more than 900,000 times.

What Is That Gooey Stuff?

Just what is that gooey stuff that drips out of your nose when you get sick? When you have a cold, blood vessels in the nose lining get leaky. Fluid leaks out of the blood vessels and mixes with mucus. This mixture contains viruses and other germs as well as dust particles that were trapped in the mucus. As the body fights the cold virus, the fluid in the nose also contains the remains of dead lining cells and the bodies of white blood cells that were killed in the battle. There may also be a bit of blood as the lining of the nose gets cracked and sore. Around the fourth day, the yucky stuff turns green or yellow from all the dead blood cells.

These body defenses help to protect us against viruses, but they also cause some of the things that make us feel so miserable. The leaky lining gets swollen, and there is less room for air to flow in and out. So it gets harder to breathe. The extra mucus dribbles out, producing a runny nose. Particles that catch on the nose hairs send messages along nerves that set off a reaction

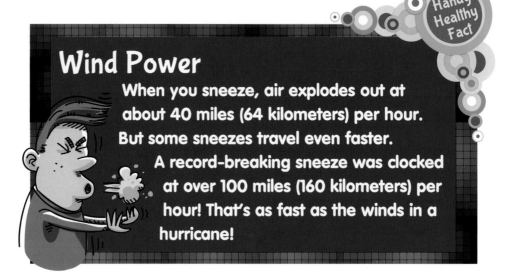

Wind Power

When you sneeze, air explodes out at about 40 miles (64 kilometers) per hour. But some sneezes travel even faster. A record-breaking sneeze was clocked at over 100 miles (160 kilometers) per hour! That's as fast as the winds in a hurricane!

in the chest muscles and make us sneeze. Some of the extra mucus that drips down the back of the throat irritates it and makes us cough. The chemicals sent out by the damaged cells can make the brain increase the body temperature, producing fever.

Some of the white blood cells produce special chemicals called antibodies. They fit the virus, just as a key fits into a lock. Antibodies may kill germs, or they may make it easier for white blood cells to eat them. Once the body has made antibodies against the cold virus, it keeps some copies even after the cold is over. They will be ready to fight if the same kind of virus invades you again.

So, if you are protected by antibodies, why can you still catch more colds? Because there are more than 200 kinds of cold viruses, and the antibodies don't work on most of them. Older people get fewer colds than children because they have fought off more cold viruses and are protected against them. And even though there are only a couple of kinds of flu viruses, they change every year. So the antibodies won't match up from one year to the next.

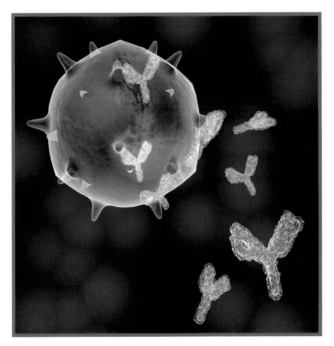

When viruses invade your body, some white blood cells produce antibodies. The antibodies (Y-shaped pink objects in this photo) attach to the viruses and help destroy them.

Diary of a Cold

Day 1
I found a new home! My old home sneezed out some viruses. They landed on her toy truck, and then her brother grabbed it. The viruses got on his hands, and then he picked his nose. Quickly my viruses dug in. Some of them settled into nice wet cells. There was plenty of food there for them. Soon the cells were making more viruses. Uh-oh! Alarms are going off. The soldiers are coming. My virus army is in for a fight!

Day 2
I think we're winning. Things are very uncomfortable, though. Some of my viruses drowned. Others were poisoned or gobbled up by those enemy soldiers. But we have them outnumbered, and we keep on making more viruses.

Day 3
It's getting hot in here, and the soldiers keep coming. We've killed a lot of them, though. My home is really complaining. He says his head hurts, and his throat hurts, and his nose is so stuffy he can hardly breathe. I wish he'd stop whining.

Day 4
It's getting wetter and wetter in here. It's hard for my viruses to find new cells before the soldiers catch them. Maybe they can escape in all that wet stuff running out of the nose.

Day 5
I'm still fighting, but things are getting very tough. The nose is still flooding.

Day 6
It's too much trouble trying to fight this. We'd better get out soon. It shouldn't be too hard to find a new home.

Day 7
Retreat! They're bringing out the big guns! They're aiming at me!

5

HOW ARE GERMS SPREAD?

When you get a cold, you might know where you got it—maybe you were playing with a friend who had been sick for a day or two. Then again, you might not have any idea where you got your cold. Maybe the store cashier passed on her cold germs when she gave you change for your purchase. But you didn't realize she had a cold.

Colds and flu are both illnesses that can spread easily from one person to another. Viruses leave the body of an infected person and get inside the body of a healthy person. How does that happen?

When you get sick, virus particles are hiding out in fluid in your eyes, nose, and throat. But how do these viruses leave your body and find a new home in

Blast From the Past

Ben Franklin slept with his windows open because he believed that fresh air prevents colds. He was right. Fresh air spreads out the virus particles in the air, making it less likely that you will breathe them in.

somebody else's? Scientists say cold viruses spread in a couple of main ways. One is through the air. When you sneeze or cough—or even when you talk—tiny droplets of moisture spray out of your nose and mouth. Cold and flu viruses can ride on those tiny droplets. If you have to cough, turn your face away from your friends so they won't catch your germs.

Another way colds and flu are spread is by hands. If you rub your eyes or wipe your nose when you are sick, you can get viruses on your hands. Then if you touch somebody else's hand, you pass on some of your germs. You can also catch a cold or flu by touching an object that was recently touched by someone with a cold or flu. Viruses can survive for hours on things like doorknobs, keyboards, telephones, dishes, books, and money.

Has anybody ever told you, "Don't go outside without a jacket or you'll catch cold"? This warning is not exactly true. (Remember, colds are caused by viruses, not by the weather.) But cold weather may make it easier for you to get sick. Cold weather weakens your body's defenses. If you come into contact with cold or flu viruses, your body's white cell defenders may

You can catch a cold by touching an object, such as a keyboard, that a sick person has touched.

Activity 1: See How Viruses Spread

Put some liquid vegetable dye in a bowl. (Use wild colors like purple, blue, or green.) Dip your fingers in the bowl to wet them with the dye. Now do some normal things, like eating a snack or bouncing a ball or drawing a picture. Every few minutes, dip your fingers in the bowl with the dye again.

After fifteen minutes, look at yourself in a mirror. How many times did you touch your face? You'll be able to tell because you will have colored spots from the vegetable dye on your skin. What else did you touch? (Hopefully you did not touch your mom's favorite white dress or the white couch!)

You probably didn't realize how often you touch your face without even thinking about it. Now can you imagine how easy it is to spread cold germs?

People catch more colds during cold weather. Wearing warm clothes can help you stay healthy.

30

be too weak to fight off the infection. It may also be easy to come down with a cold or flu when you are too hot, very tired, or if you have not been eating very well.

People who smoke cigarettes may have worse colds than nonsmokers. Children of parents who smoke tend to have more colds, and other health problems, too. Pollution and allergies also put a heavy load on the defenses in your nose and throat and may lead to really bad colds. In general, the more stress you have, the greater your chances are of getting sick.

Handy Healthy Fact

Monday Blues

People get more colds on Mondays than any other day. Could it be that we do not want to go back to school or work on Monday? Well, maybe. But remember, colds take a couple of days to get started. It takes time for those viruses to multiply. So the cold that you notice on Monday was probably caught the week before, from somebody you met who had a cold.

6

TREATING COLDS AND FLU

What should you do when you get sick? Are there medications you can take to feel better? People go to doctors more for colds and flu than for any other reason. Unfortunately, doctors can't do much for someone with a cold or the flu. Of course, there are plenty of cold and flu remedies that you can buy in the supermarket or drugstore. Medications can make you feel a little better, but most of them don't fight the viruses that are making you sick.

Some people ask doctors to give them a shot of penicillin or some other antibiotic to get rid of a bad cold or the flu. Antibiotics are good drugs for diseases caused by bacteria, but they do not work on viruses. In fact, taking antibiotics too often may even be harmful,

This doctor is examining a girl who has a cold.

because they may help to breed super-germs that can't be killed by medications.

However, antiviral drugs—drugs that do kill viruses—may be used to treat the flu. These drugs help to lessen the symptoms and make them go away faster. But they have to be taken within the first two days after the symptoms appear to work well. Relenza® and Tamiflu® are common antiviral drugs.

Antibiotics can be used to treat pneumonia caused by bacteria. This infection should be treated as soon as possible. Sometimes, the infection develops so quickly that the damage to the lungs and other organs cannot be repaired even if the drugs wipe out the bacteria.

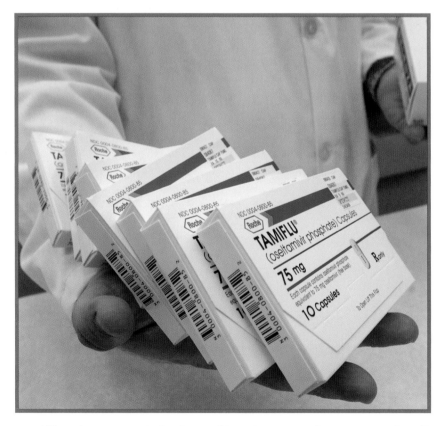

Tamiflu® is an antiviral medication used to treat the flu.

Aspirin is a popular remedy for treating illnesses like colds and flu—it helps aches and pains and headaches. But not everyone should take aspirin. In the 1970s, scientists found that children who took aspirin for a viral illness were more likely to develop Reye's syndrome, which damages the liver and nervous system. Some even died! Fortunately, Reye's syndrome is very rare. But today, doctors tell parents to give their children acetaminophen or ibuprofen instead of aspirin when they have colds and flu.

Most people treat their cold and flu symptoms at home. But some people may need to see a doctor. Colds and especially flu can be very harmful to babies, people older than seventy, pregnant women, and people who have problems with their heart and lungs. These people should call the doctor if they have:

If anyone, especially a child has a high fever for several days, he or she should see a doctor.

- symptoms that are very serious or go on for more than a week
- a fever above 102 degrees Fahrenheit (39 degrees Celsius) for more than two days
- constant coughing that prevents sleeping
- coughing that makes colored mucus for more than two days
- bad headaches, stiff neck, swollen glands, or a rash.

Colds and flu may sometimes lead to other infections such as bronchitis, tonsillitis, sinusitis, ear infections, and pneumonia. These are bacterial infections that can develop when the body is weakened by fighting cold or flu viruses. Unlike viral infections, bacterial infections can be treated with medications.

For most people with colds and flu, the only thing doctors can do is tell them to get some rest, drink plenty of fluids, keep warm, and take over-the-counter drugs to treat cold or flu symptoms. These medications can help dry up a runny nose, stop coughing, and soothe a sore throat and headache.

There are dozens of over-the-counter drugs designed to treat cold symptoms.

Some people think that taking extra vitamin C and the mineral zinc when cold symptoms first appear may prevent the cold from developing, or make it much shorter and milder.

Chicken Soup! Mmm Mmm Good!

In the twelfth century, a Jewish philosopher named Maimonides said that chicken soup is good for colds. He may have been right. In 1978, Dr. Marvin Sackner of Mount Sinai Hospital in Miami Beach, Florida, found that chicken soup helped to clear the mucus from a stuffy nose much faster than other liquids.

SOUP

7

PREVENTING COLDS AND FLU

Is it possible to prevent colds? Unfortunately, there is no vaccine that can keep you from catching colds. Since there are hundreds of cold viruses, it would be really hard to protect you against all of them.

On the bright side, there is a flu vaccine. Every year, millions of people get flu shots. But they have to get a new one each year because flu viruses change each season. Medical experts use research to predict which flu viruses are going around. Then vaccines are made to protect against them.

Although there is no vaccine for the common cold, there is a vaccine for the flu.

Ouchless Flu Vaccine

Most people do not like getting shots, especially kids. But in 2003, a new kind of vaccine was approved—FluMist®. This vaccine gets sprayed in a person's nostrils. Unlike the flu shot, which contains killed viruses, FluMist is a live, but weakened vaccine. The viruses are weakened so that they do not multiply in the body. But they may cause flu symptoms in some people. Therefore, FluMist cannot be given to people with serious health problems, such as AIDS or cancer, or those with respiratory conditions, such as asthma.

This vaccine is given to a patient by spraying it into her nostrils.

Many people do not get the flu vaccine every year. And since there is no vaccine against colds, that means lots and lots of people still get sick every year. Is there anything we can do about it?

The only sure way to keep from getting sick is to stay away from people who are sick and anything they may have touched. That's not easy. Imagine what your life would be like if you had to stay away from your sick mom or dad for a whole week! Or if they had to stay

Cover Your Mouth

How many times have you heard, "Cover your mouth when you cough"? Covering your mouth when you cough or sneeze is supposed to be polite. After all, you don't want to spread your germs out into the air that other people are breathing. But coughing into your hand leaves germs there— germs that may spread to somebody else through touching. So should you cover or not cover? The best answer: Cover your mouth and then wash your hands!

away from you when you were sick! But there are things you can do to prevent colds and the flu without having to hide from sick people.

First, you need to cut down the chances for spreading colds or the flu. To keep cold or flu viruses from getting to you, try not to touch people who have these illnesses, wash your hands regularly, and always wash your hands before touching your eyes or nose. (Washing your hands won't kill the cold viruses, but it will wash them down the drain.) If you are the one

If you eat well and exercise regularly, you are less likely to catch colds.

who's sick, washing your hands often can help keep you from spreading your viruses to others.

Another important way you can keep from getting sick is to have a healthy lifestyle. You can do this by eating well, exercising regularly, getting enough rest, and practicing clean habits (washing your hands and keeping your body, clothes, food, and dishes clean). If you are healthy and strong, then your body's defenses will be strong enough to fight off invading viruses.

Some health experts believe that taking vitamin C can help keep your body strong enough to fight off diseases. Other people say you do not need to take extra vitamins because a balanced diet gives you all you need to be healthy. The problem is that you may not always eat what you should.

It's unlikely that we'll ever be able to one day wipe out colds with a cold vaccine or get everyone to get a flu shot every year. So getting sick is just a part of life. Fortunately, scientists continue to search for more effective ways to treat and possibly prevent colds and flu.

GLOSSARY

antibiotics—Medicines that kill bacteria.

antibodies—Special germ-fighting chemicals produced by white blood cells.

antiviral drugs—Medicines that kill viruses.

bronchitis—An infection of the bronchi, the hollow tubes leading from the nose and mouth down into the lungs.

electron microscope—A special kind of microscope that uses beams of electrons (particles with a negative electric charge) rather than light rays to make pictures of very tiny objects.

mucus—A gooey liquid produced by cells in the lining of the nose and breathing passages.

pneumonia—An infection of the lungs.

respiratory system—The breathing passages and lungs.

Reye's syndrome—An illness that damages the liver and respiratory system. It may develop when young people with a viral infection take aspirin.

rhinitis—A stuffed-up, runny nose.

rhinovirus—One of the main kinds of viruses that cause colds.

sinusitis—An infection of the lining of the sinuses, air-filled spaces inside the bones of the skull.

tonsillitis—An infection of the tonsils, masses of germ-fighting tissue at the back of the throat.

vaccine—A substance that stimulates the body's disease-fighting cells to produce antibodies against a particular kind of germ.

virus—The smallest kind of germ, which cannot be seen through even an ordinary microscope.

vitamin C—A nutrient chemical found in fresh fruits and vegetables that helps to keep the body's disease-fighting cells strong and active.

white blood cells—Disease-fighting cells that travel in the blood and squeeze through the tiny gaps between cells in the body tissues.

LEARN MORE

Books

Burgan, Michael. *Developing Flu Vaccines*. Chicago: Raintree, 2011.

Cobb, Vicki. *Your Body Battles a Cold*. Minneapolis, Minn.: Millbrook Press, 2009.

Grady, Denise. *Deadly Invaders: Virus Outbreaks Around the World, From Marburg Fever to Avian Flu*. Boston: Kingfisher, 2006.

Hoffmann, Gretchen. *The Flu*. Tarrytown, N.Y.: Marshall Cavendish Benchmark, 2007.

Web Sites

Nemours Foundation. "Chilling Out With Colds." <http://kidshealth.org/kid/ill_injure/sick/colds.html>

Nemours Foundation. "The Flu." <http://kidshealth.org/kid/h1n1_center/flu-basics/flu.html>

INDEX